ANNE GEDDES

my *first five* years™

A journal of early childhood

GEDDES GROUP

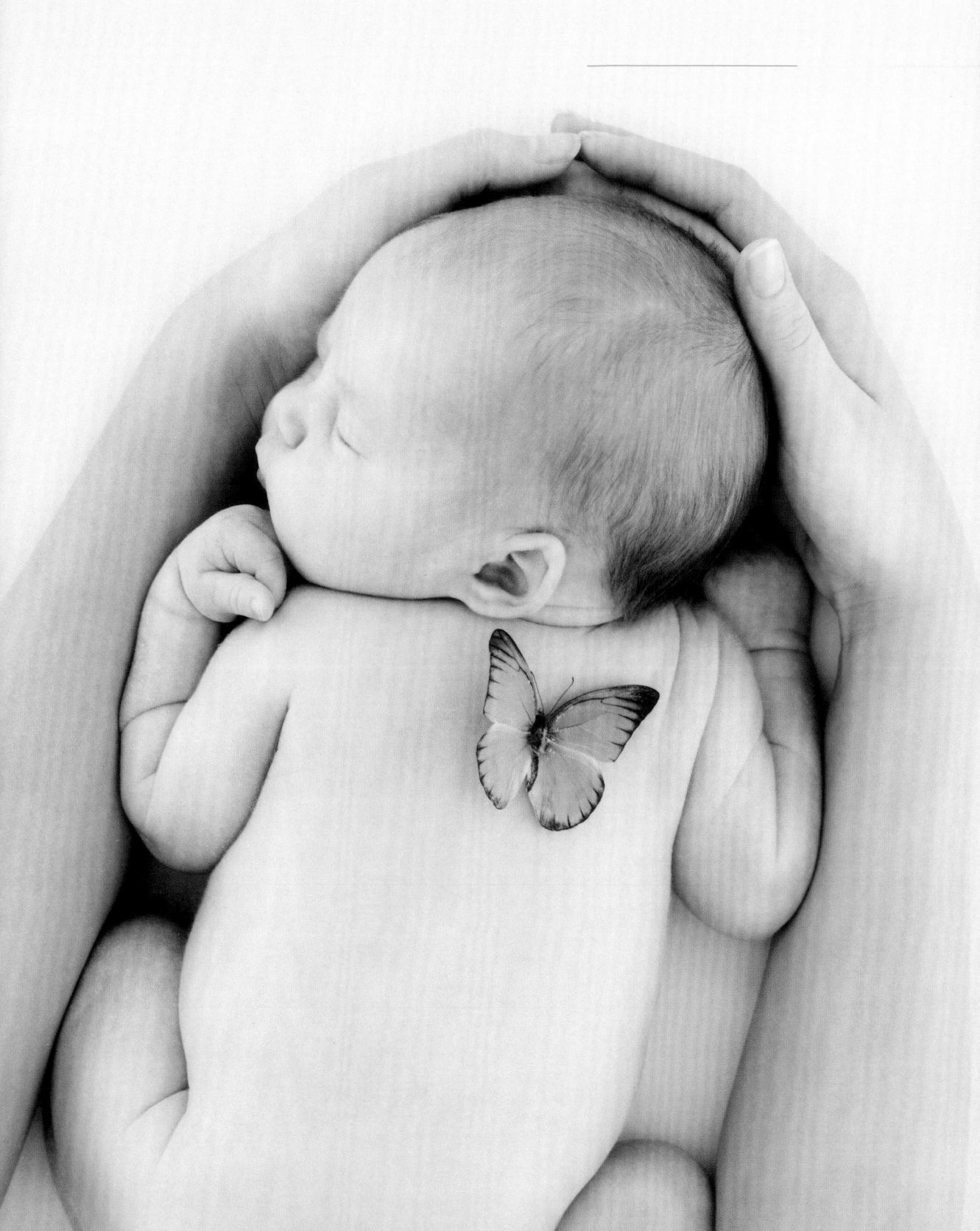

This journal belongs to

⋯⋯⋯⋯⋯⋯⋯⋯⋯⋯⋯⋯⋯⋯⋯⋯⋯⋯⋯

With love from

⋯⋯⋯⋯⋯⋯⋯⋯⋯⋯⋯⋯⋯⋯⋯⋯⋯⋯⋯

Contents

a mementos envelope is included on the inside back cover

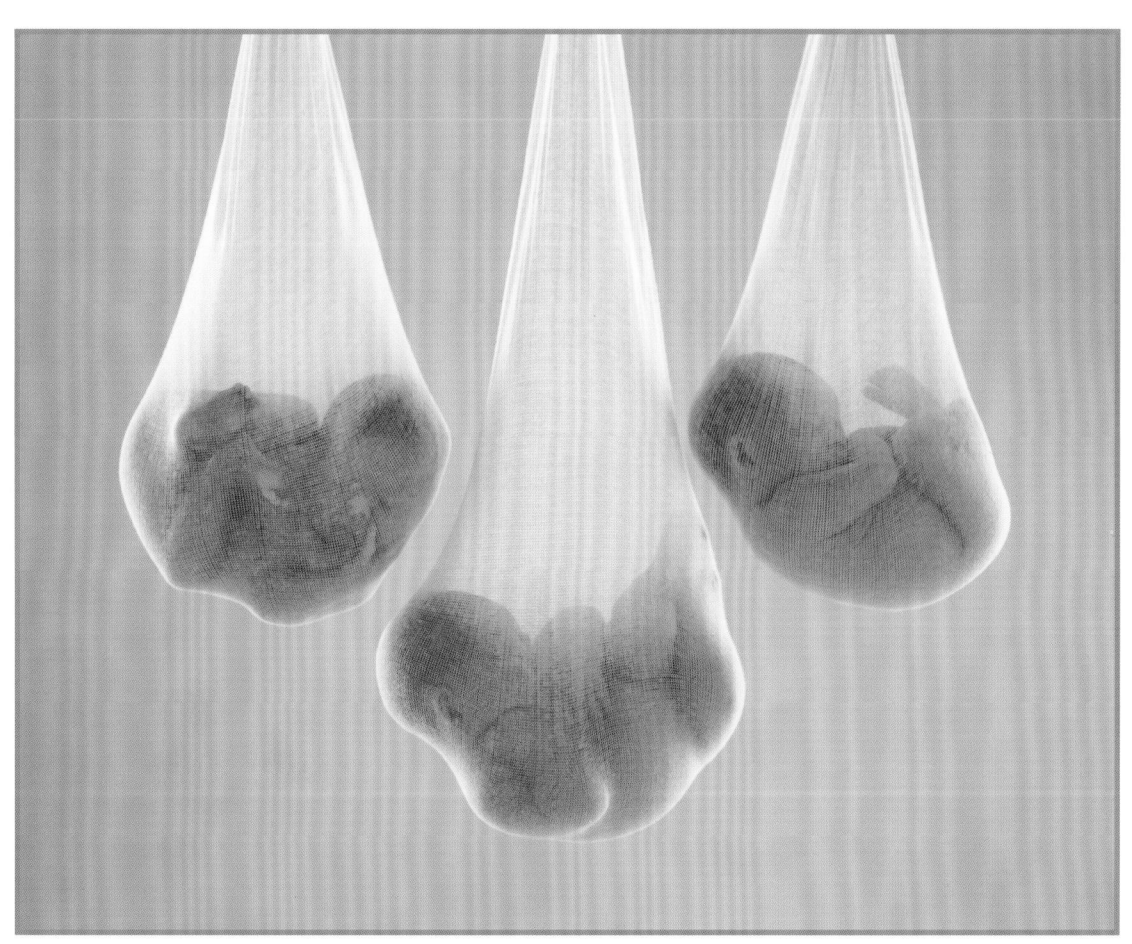

"This is where we start to make a better world."

Anne

My Parents

space for photograph

name _____ name _____

_____ _____

date of birth _____ date of birth _____

place of birth _____ place of birth _____

_____ _____

_____ _____

brothers and sisters _____ brothers and sisters _____

_____ _____

_____ _____

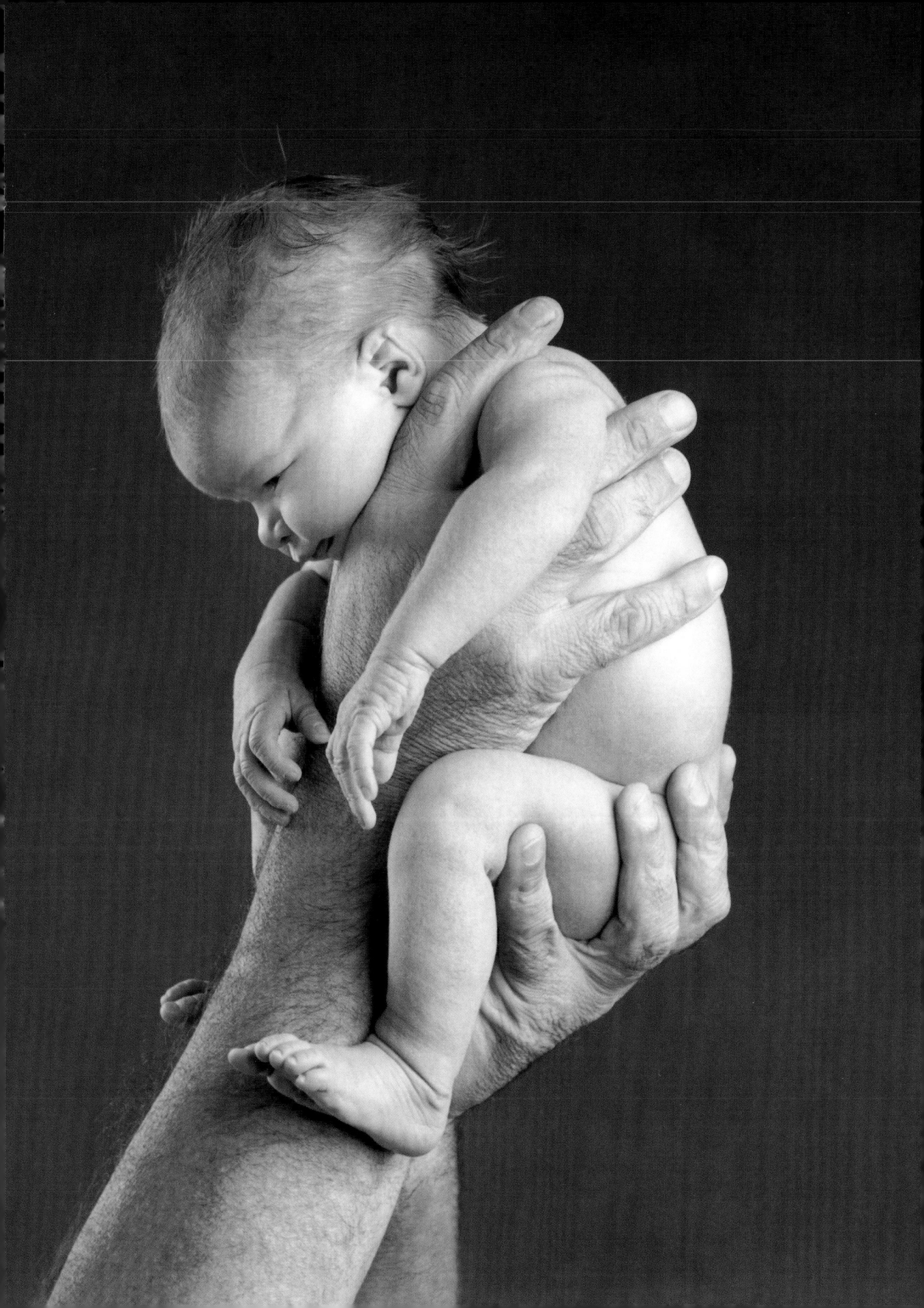

Before My Arrival

date pregnancy confirmed

due date

space for ultrasound

my mother's age when she was expecting me

how my mother found out she was expecting me

the person my parents told first was

a funny moment from my mother's pregnancy was

foods my mother craved were

my parents' thoughts and feelings

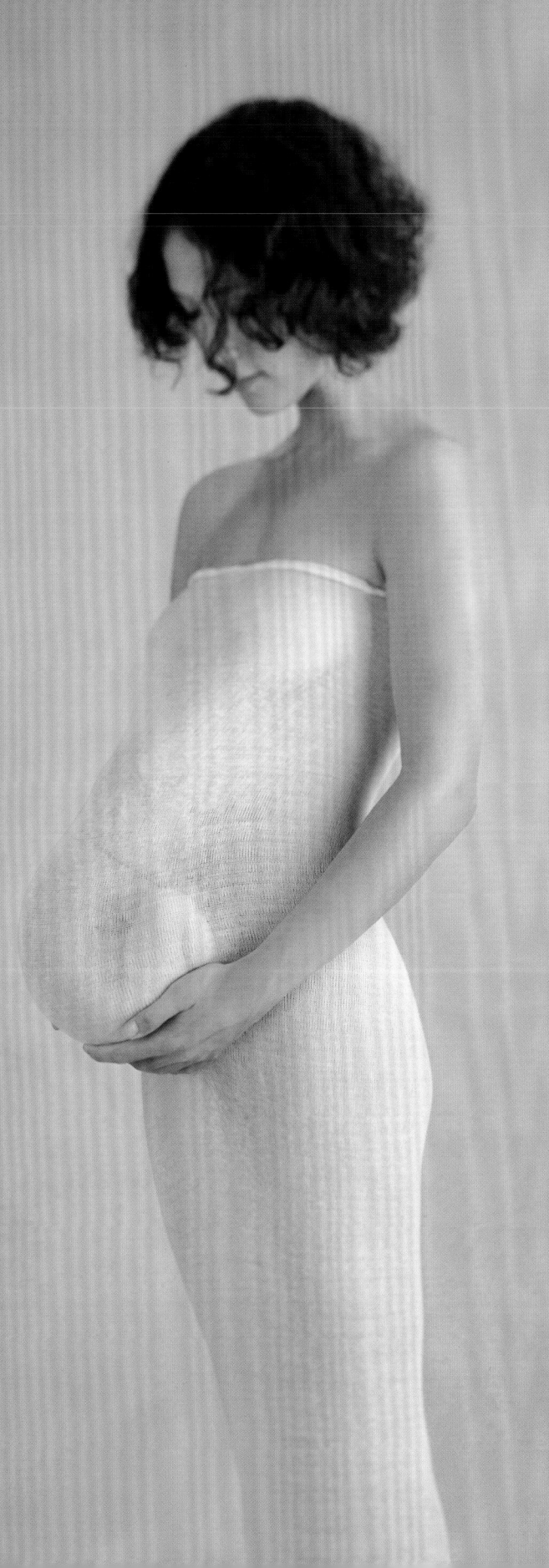

My First Photograph

My Birth

I was born on

the time was

my birth lasted

the place I was born

I was delivered by

the people present were

I weighed

I measured

my eye color

my hair color

my blood type

I looked like

my star sign

the chinese year

my birthstone

my birth flower

Special Messages

from my parents

_____

_____

_____

_____

_____

_____

_____

from my family

_____

_____

_____

_____

_____

_____

_____

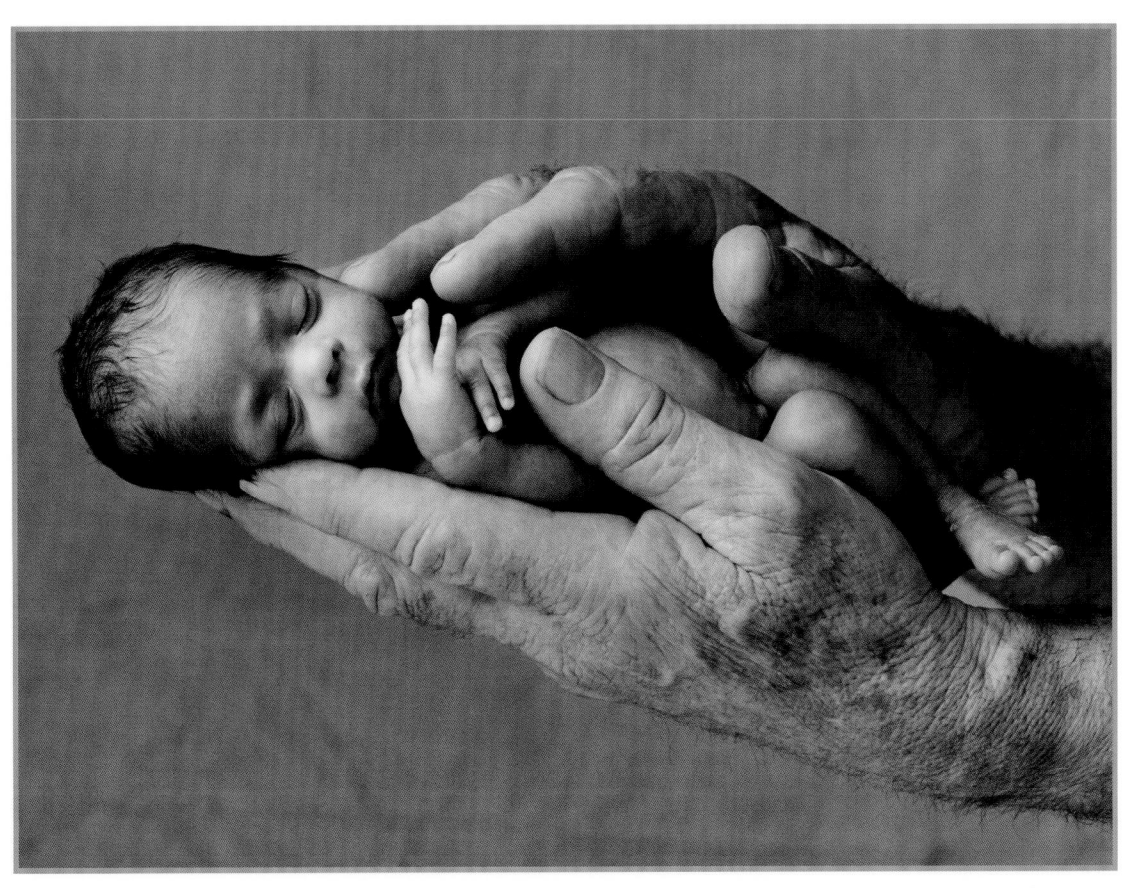

"Over the years I have come to realize that newborn babies
are very powerful little people."

Anne.

Mementos

ultrasound, birth announcement, hospital tag

Mementos

gift cards, emails, pressed flowers, birthday horoscope

My First Visitors

name

message

name

message

name

message

My First Visitors

name

message

name

message

name

message

The World When I Arrived

the President was _____

significant events that happened were _____

_____

_____

the local news headline was _____

_____

the weather was _____

the number one song was _____

the blockbuster movies were _____

the fashion trends were _____

famous people who share my birthday are _____

a quart of milk cost _____

a newspaper cost _____

music my parents were listening to was _____

_____

_____

the latest technology available was _____

_____

Newspaper Clippings

My Photographs

My Homecoming

the date I came home _____

my address _____

_____

_____

the people waiting to welcome me were _____

_____

how I reacted to being home _____

_____

_____

my family's thoughts and feelings that day _____

_____

_____

_____

_____

_____

_____

My Homecoming

reactions from my brothers and sisters

_____

_____

_____

reactions from my pets

_____

my first night home

_____

house guests or helpers

_____

how I fed in the first week

_____

how I slept in the first week

_____

how my parents felt in the first week

_____

_____

_____

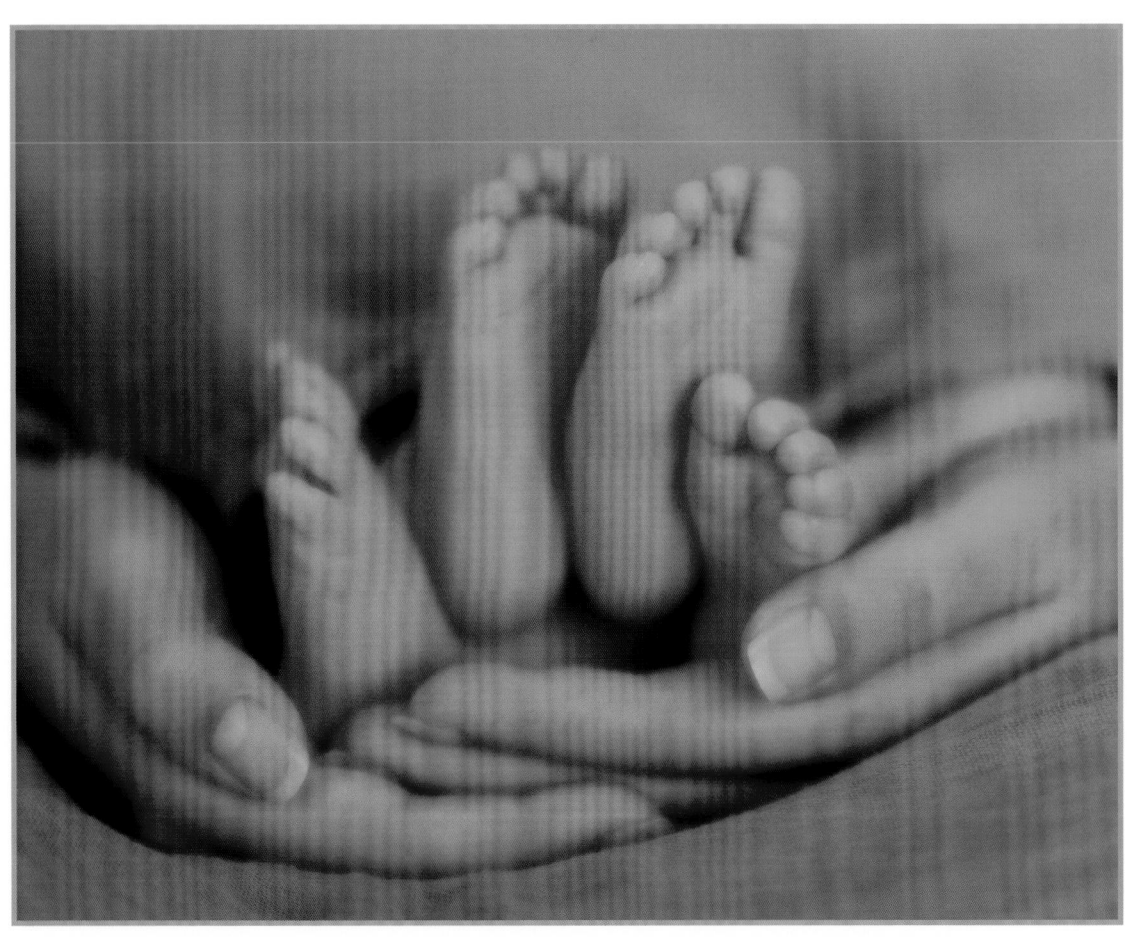

"In any country in the world, the emotional connection between a mother and her newborn is equally powerful."

Anne.

My Name

my full name is

my name was chosen by

my name means

my nicknames are

ceremonies celebrating my birth

memorable moments

my parents' favorite names for a girl

my parents' favorite names for a boy

My Family Tree

attach grandparent's photograph

attach grandparent's photograph

attach grandparent's photograph

attach grandparent's photograph

attach parent's photograph

attach parent's photograph

attach own photograph

My Photographs

Three Months

my weight _____

my length _____

what I am like _____

_____

_____

_____

_____

what makes me smile _____

_____

_____

_____

what I like doing _____

_____

_____

_____

_____

Six Months

my weight

my length

what I am like

what I can do now

sounds I make

My Photographs

My Milestones

I first smiled

I first laughed

I first grasped a toy

I first slept through the night

I first held my head up

I first rolled over

I first sat up

I first crawled

I first stood up

I first walked

I first ate solid foods

I first tried finger foods

my first tooth

my first word

other milestones

Nine Months

my weight _____

my length _____

what I am like _____

_____

_____

_____

_____

what makes me laugh _____

_____

_____

_____

_____

what I like doing _____

_____

_____

_____

_____

_____

My Photographs

My First Birthday

my weight _____

my height _____

my first words _____

_____

_____

_____

what's happening in my world _____

_____

_____

_____

what I am like _____

_____

_____

_____

what I like doing _____

_____

_____

_____

"Babies speak a universal language."

Anne.

My Photographs

My First Birthday

about my party

where we celebrated it

_____

who was there

_____

_____

_____

_____

special gifts

_____

_____

_____

_____

my first birthday cake

_____

memorable moments

_____

_____

_____

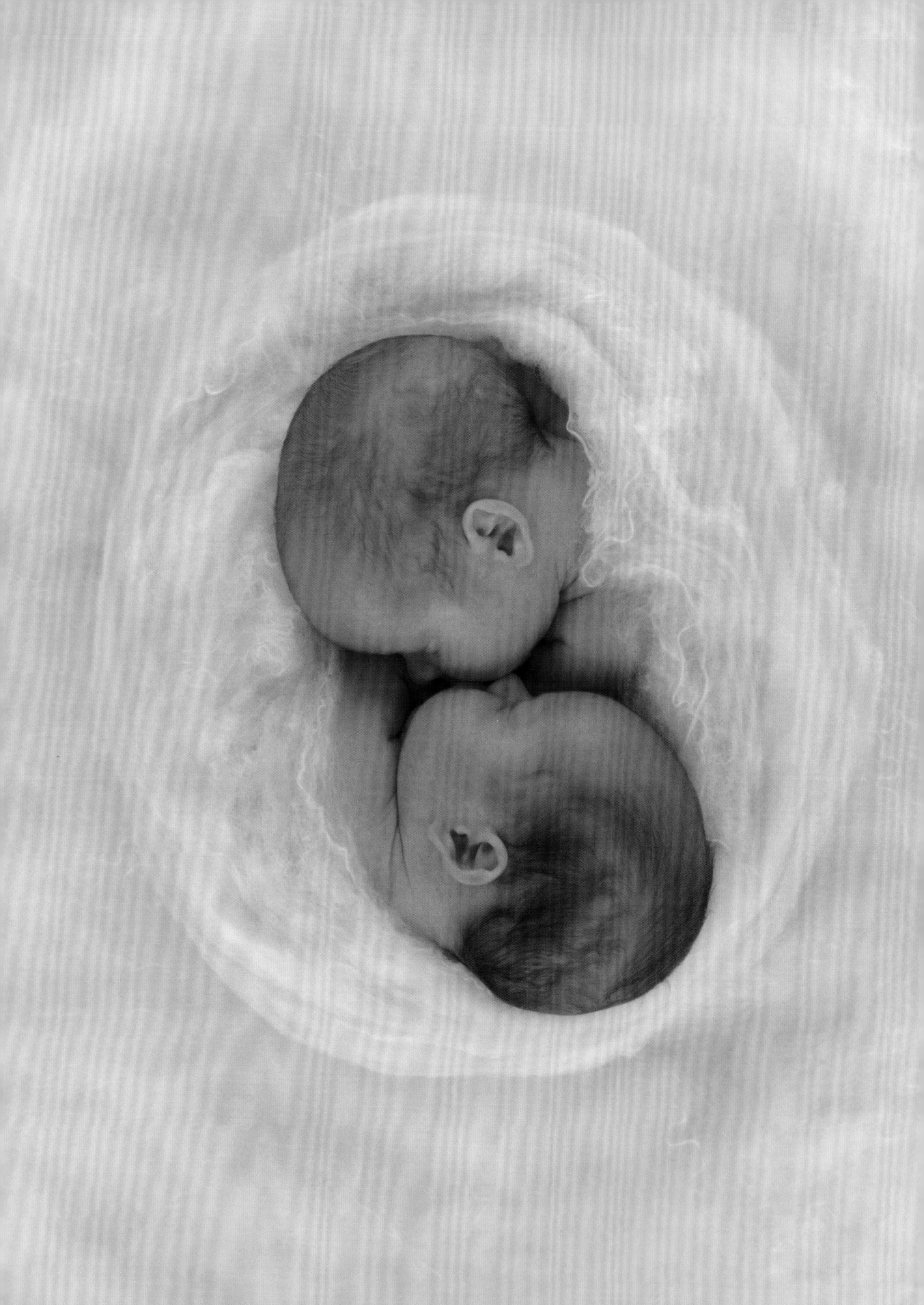

My Favorites

now I'm one

food

_____

_____

music

_____

_____

nursery rhymes

_____

_____

animals

_____

_____

books

_____

_____

toys

_____

_____

friends

_____

_____

activities

_____

_____

I really don't like

_____

_____

My Second Birthday

my weight _____

my height _____

what I am like _____

_____

_____

_____

_____

some words I can say _____

_____

_____

_____

_____

what I like doing _____

_____

_____

_____

_____

My Photographs

My Second Birthday

about my party

where we celebrated it

who was there

special gifts

my birthday cake

memorable moments

My Favorites

now I'm two

food
_____

_____

clothes
_____

_____

music
_____

_____

animals
_____

_____

books
_____

_____

toys
_____

_____

friends
_____

_____

activities
_____

_____

I really don't like
_____

_____

"There's something incredibly special about a new life." Anne.

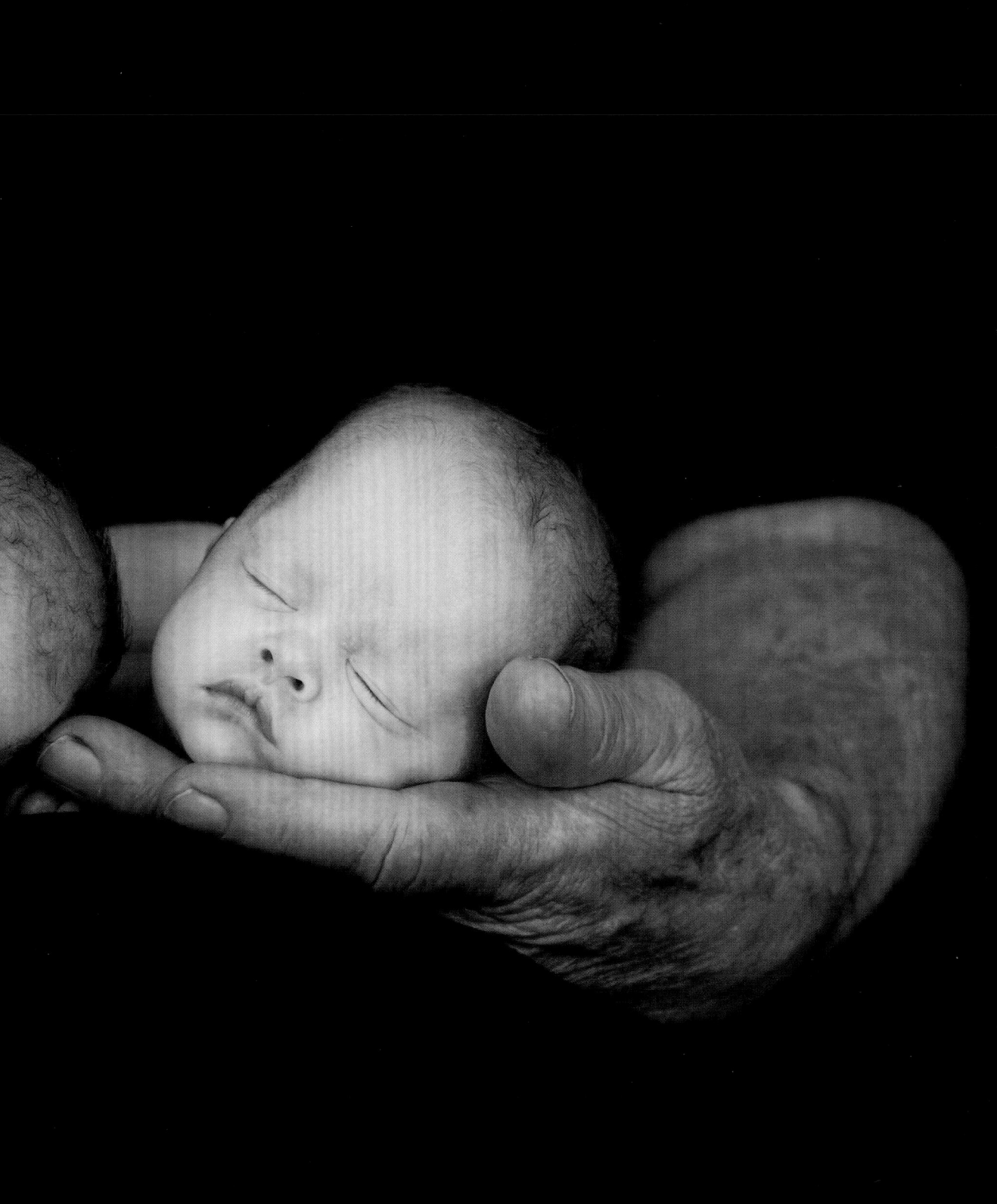

My Third Birthday

my weight _____

my height _____

what I am like _____

_____

_____

_____

what's happening in my world _____

_____

_____

_____

how I spend my time _____

_____

_____

_____

My Photographs

My Third Birthday

about my party

where we celebrated it

who was there

special gifts

my birthday cake

memorable moments

My Favorites

now I'm three

food

clothes

music

games

animals

books

toys

activities

I really don't like

"They are our future — so pure, so perfect, so innocent,
and with so much promise."

Anne.

Kindergarten

I started on

my kindergarten is called

my friends are

what I like to do there

comments

My Fourth Birthday

my weight _____

my height _____

what I am like _____

_____

_____

_____

_____

_____

what's happening in my world _____

_____

_____

_____

_____

_____

_____

My Photographs

My Fourth Birthday

about my party

where we celebrated it

_____

who was there

_____

_____

_____

_____

special gifts

_____

_____

_____

my birthday cake

_____

memorable moments

_____

_____

_____

My Favorites

now I'm four

cartoon

toast topping

song

animals

books

toys

games

activities

word/saying

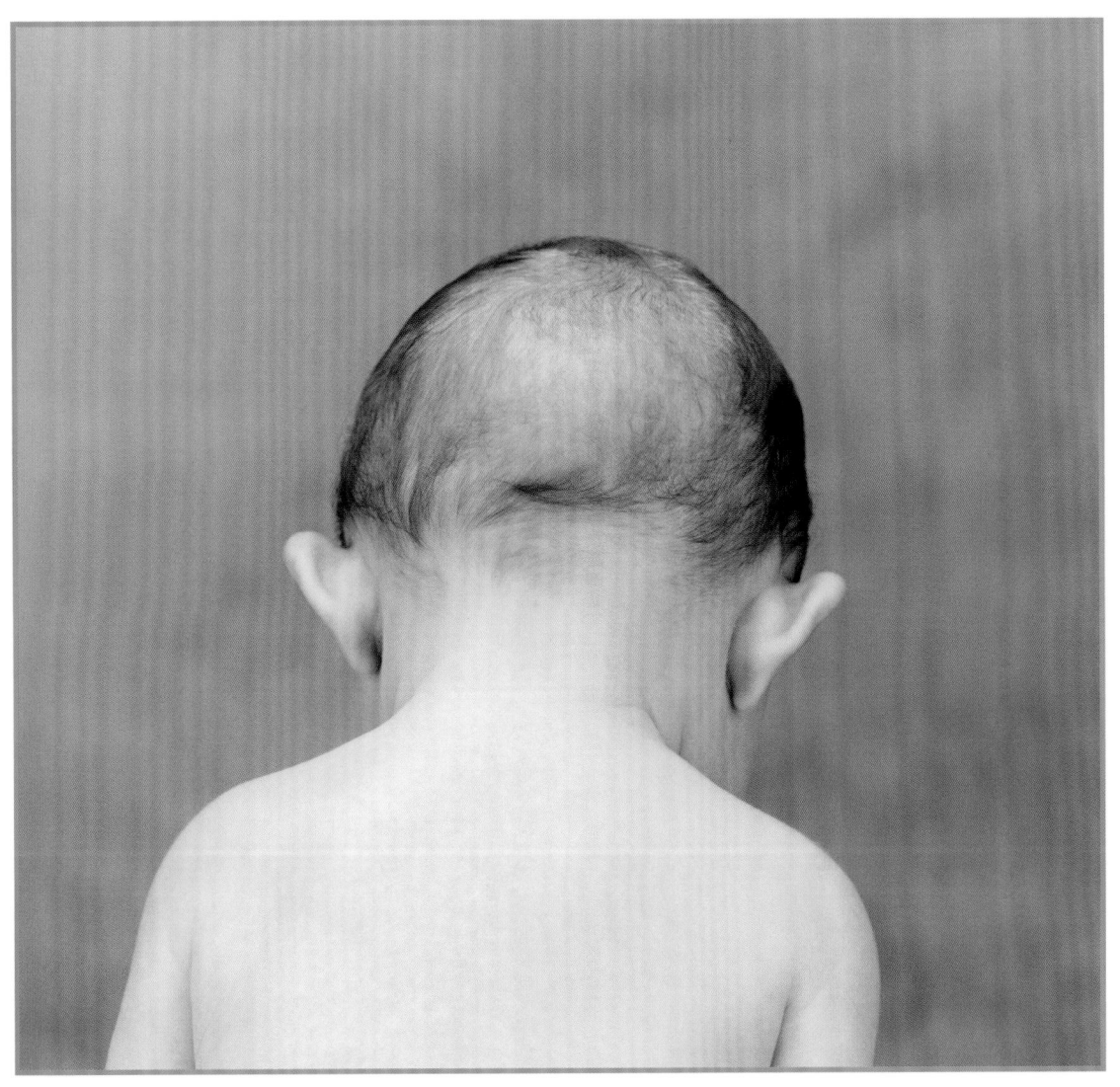

"The sheer simplicity of the image speaks volumes for the delicate vulnerability of small children."

My Fifth Birthday

my weight _____

my height _____

what I am like _____

_____

_____

_____

_____

_____

_____

what's happening in my world _____

_____

_____

_____

_____

_____

My Photographs

My Fifth Birthday

about my party

where we celebrated it

_____

_____

who was there

_____

_____

_____

_____

special gifts

_____

_____

_____

_____

my birthday cake

_____

memorable moments

_____

_____

_____

My Favorites

now I'm five

color

superhero

snack

books

toys

games

special friends

hobby

television program

"Sometimes the best flowers arrive unexpectedly." Anne.

Special Occasions

Christening, Baptism, Naming Day, Thanksgiving, 4th of July, Vacation

the special occasion was

where we celebrated it

about the occasion

space for photograph

Special Occasions

Christening, Baptism, Naming Day, Thanksgiving, 4th of July, Vacation

the special occasion was

where we celebrated it

about the occasion

space for photograph

Special Occasions

Christening, Baptism, Naming Day, Thanksgiving, 4th of July, Vacation

the special occasion was

where we celebrated it

about the occasion

space for photograph

Special Occasions

Christening, Baptism, Naming Day, Thanksgiving, 4th of July, Vacation

the special occasion was

where we celebrated it

about the occasion

space for photograph

Special Occasions

Christening, Baptism, Naming Day, Thanksgiving, 4th of July, Vacation

the special occasion was

where we celebrated it

about the occasion

space for photograph

Special Occasions

Christening, Baptism, Naming Day, Thanksgiving, 4th of July, Vacation

the special occasion was

where we celebrated it

about the occasion

space for photograph

My Photographs

School

I started on

my school is called

my teacher is

on my first day I

my friends are

comments

My Drawings

My Drawings

My Writing

I could recite the alphabet

I started to write

I began to read

my writing

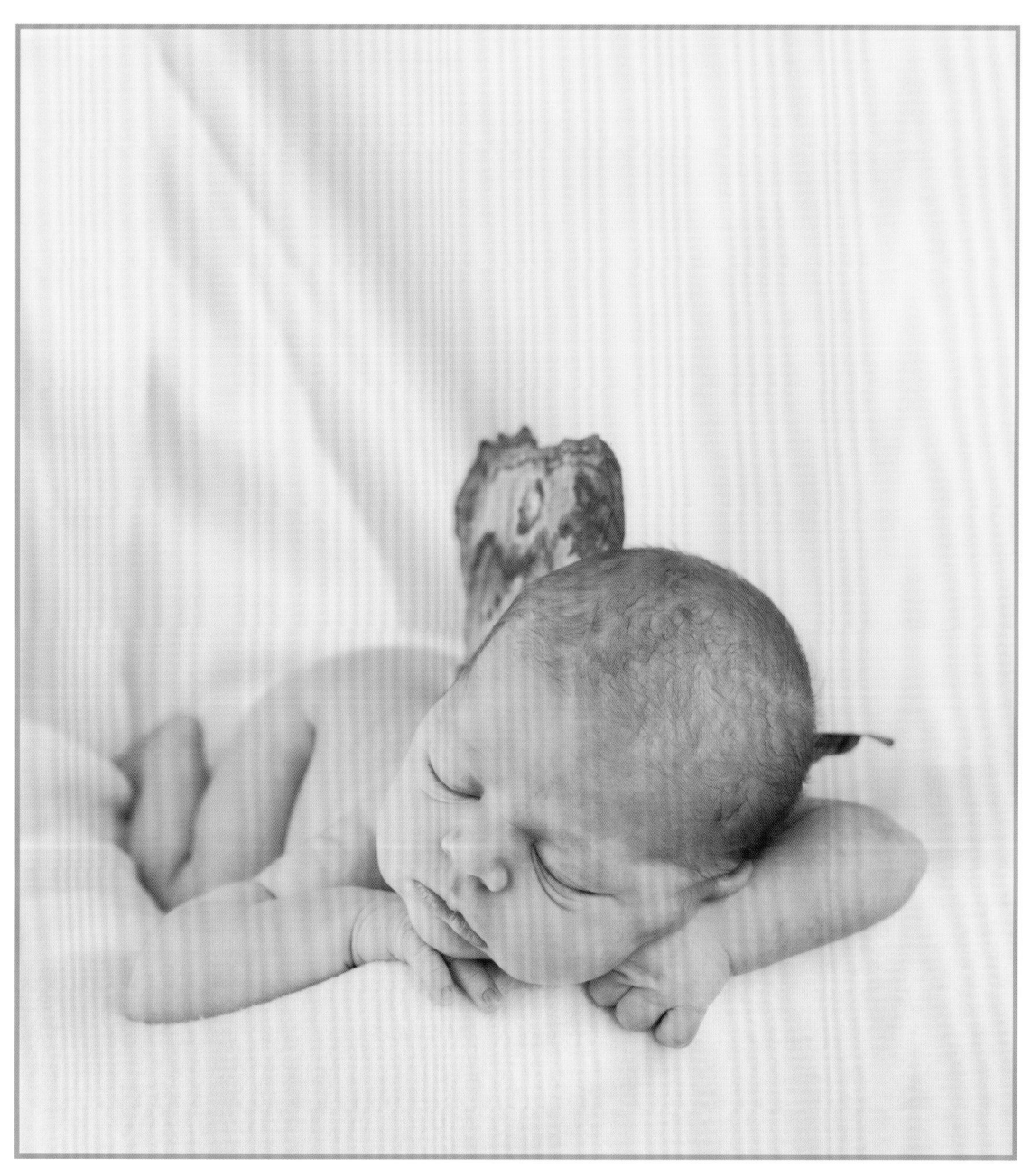

"Indeed babies reach out to people on all levels, emotional, physical and spiritual."

Anne.

My Friends

photographs and names of the friends I've made in my first five years

My Friends

photographs and names of the friends I've made in my first five years

My Friends

photographs and names of the friends I've made in my first five years

My Friends

photographs and names of the friends I've made in my first five years

My Height

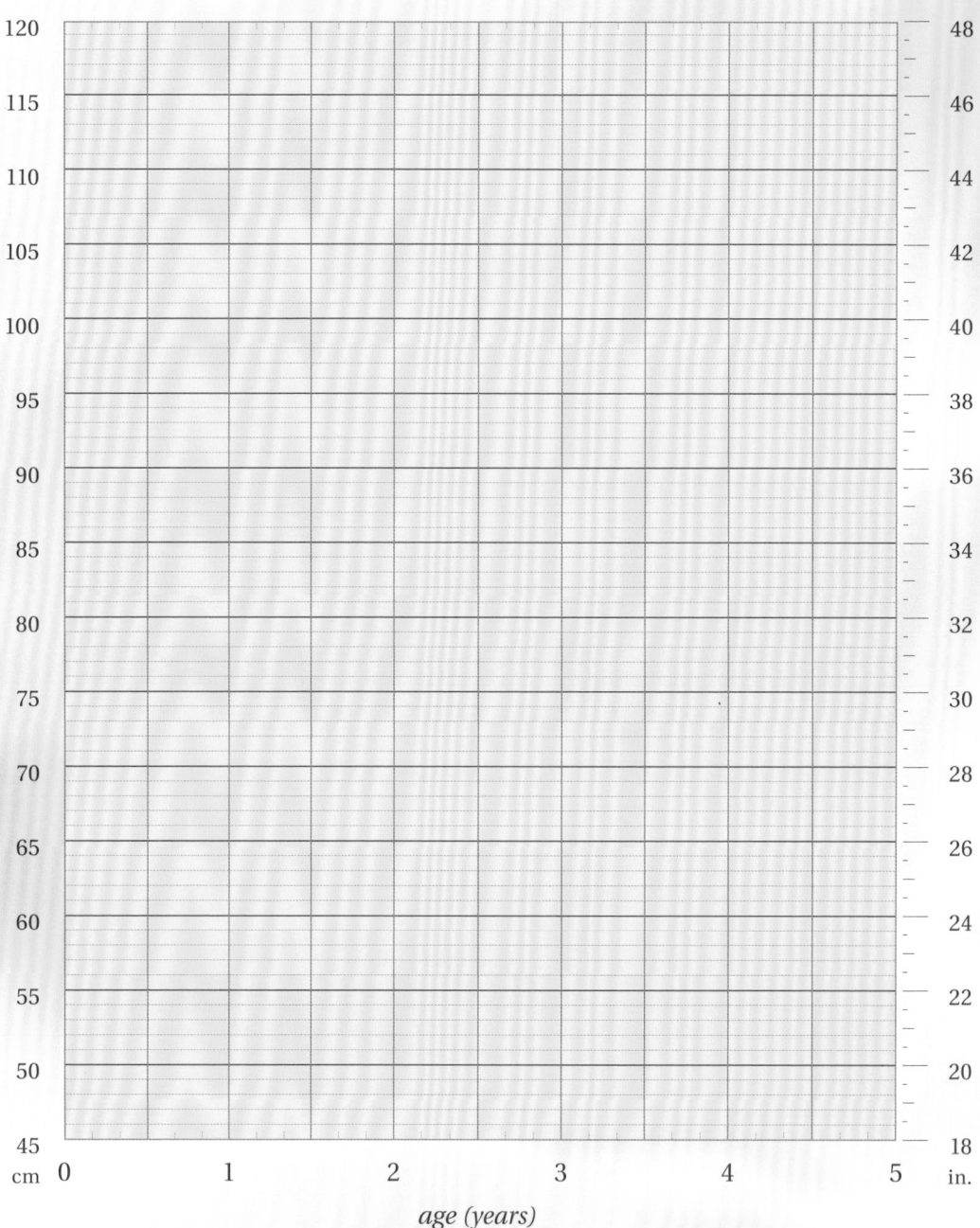

age (years)

My Weight

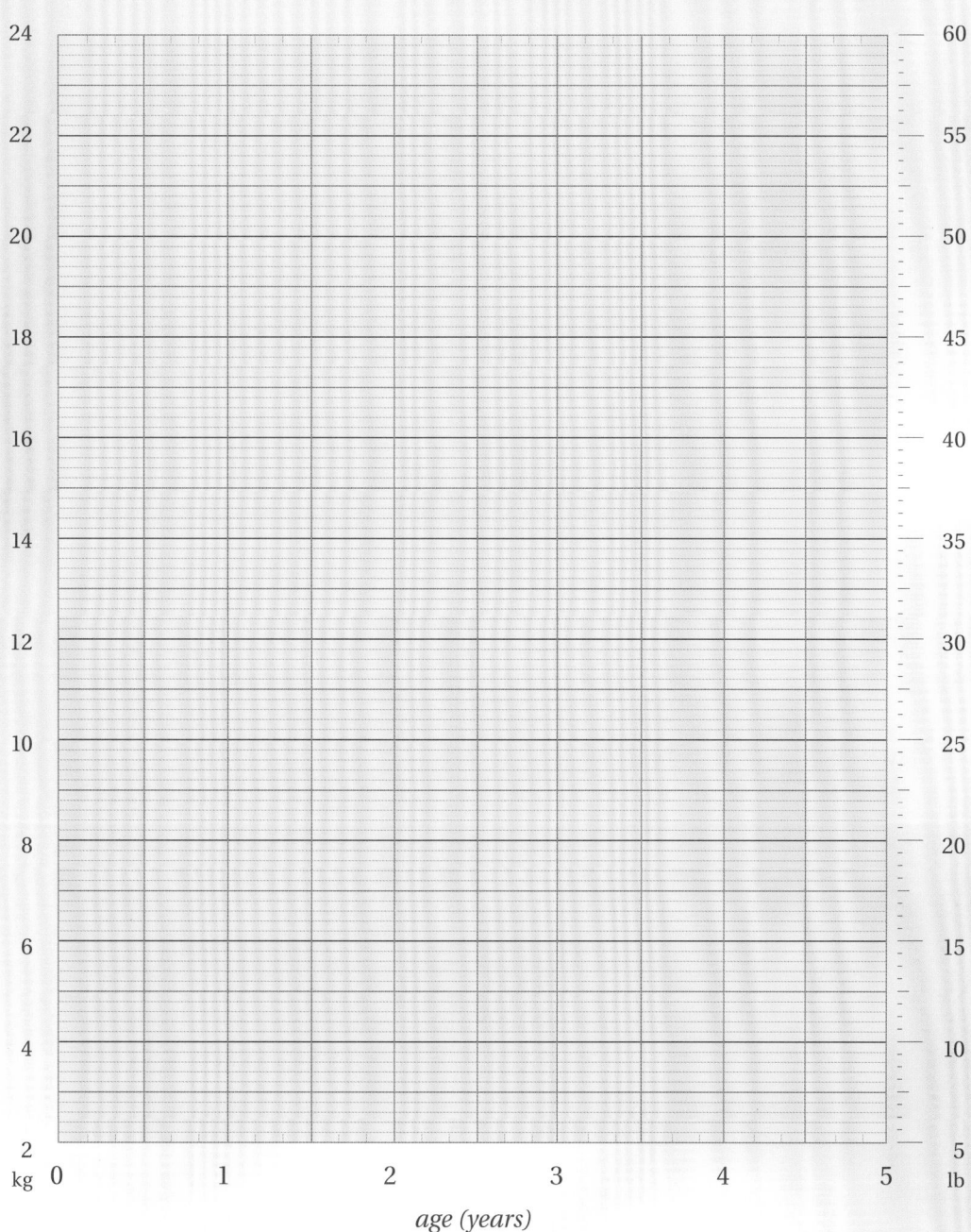

My Health

my health visitor is

my doctor is

my age at first health appointment

my health appointment results

my age at second health appointment

my health appointment results

my age at third health appointment

my health appointment results

my age at fourth health appointment

my health appointment results

My Health

vaccinations	age	date

allergies

illnesses

comments

My Health

my first illness was

how I reacted

how my parents coped

I began teething at age

the person who found my first tooth was

how I slept whilst teething

how my parents comforted me whilst teething

The Tooth Fairy's Page

upper jaw dates

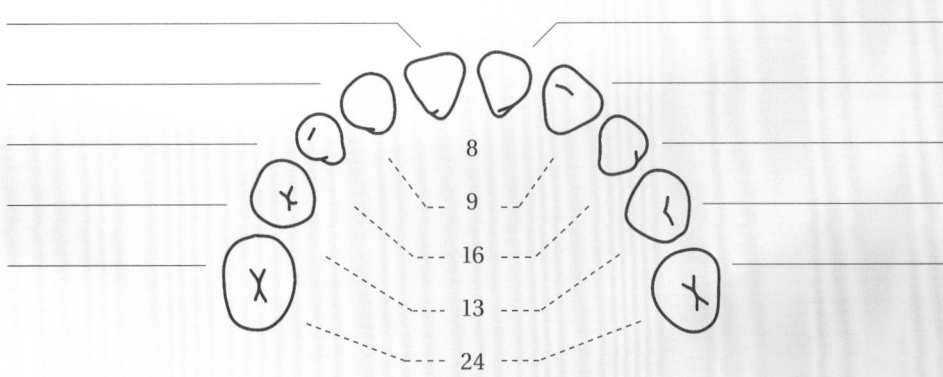

```
8
9
16
13
24
```

months

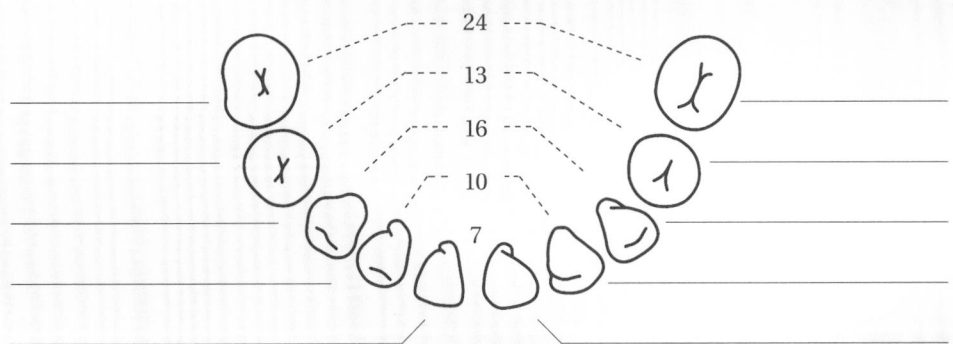

```
24
13
16
10
7
```

lower jaw dates

I lost my first tooth _____

my second tooth _____

the tooth fairy left me _____

visits to the dentist _____

_____

89

My Handprints

at birth

at five years

My Footprints

at birth

at five years

Birthstones

JANUARY	Garnet – constancy, truth
FEBRUARY	Amethyst – sincerity, humility
MARCH	Aquamarine – courage, energy
APRIL	Diamond – innocence, success
MAY	Emerald – tranquillity
JUNE	Pearl – preciousness, purity
JULY	Ruby – freedom from care, chastity
AUGUST	Moonstone – joy
SEPTEMBER	Sapphire – hope, chastity
OCTOBER	Opal – reflecting every mood
NOVEMBER	Topaz – fidelity, loyalty
DECEMBER	Turquoise – love, success

Flowers

JANUARY	Snowdrop – pure and gentle
FEBRUARY	Carnation – bold and brave
MARCH	Violet – modest
APRIL	Lily – virtuous
MAY	Hawthorn – bright and hopeful
JUNE	Rose – beautiful
JULY	Daisy – wide-eyed and innocent
AUGUST	Poppy – peaceful
SEPTEMBER	Morning Glory – easily contented
OCTOBER	Cosmos – ambitious
NOVEMBER	Chrysanthemum – cheeky and cheerful
DECEMBER	Holly – full of foresight

"My own desire is that my imagery will help to create a strong platform of hope and promise for humanity and the future."

Anne.

Star Signs

CAPRICORN
22 December – 20 January
Resourceful, self-sufficient and responsible

AQUARIUS
21 January – 18 February
Cares greatly for others, very emotional under a cool exterior

PISCES
19 February – 19 March
Imaginative, sympathetic and tolerant

ARIES
20 March – 20 April
Brave, energetic and loyal

TAURUS
21 April – 21 May
Sensible, loves peace and stability

GEMINI
22 May – 21 June
Unpredictable, lively, charming and witty

CANCER
22 June – 22 July
Loves security and comfort

LEO
23 July – 23 August
Idealistic, romantic, honorable and loyal

VIRGO
24 August – 23 September
Shy, sensitive and values knowledge

LIBRA
24 September – 23 October
Diplomatic, full of charm and style

SCORPIO
24 October – 22 November
Compassionate, proud and determined

SAGITTARIUS
23 November – 21 December
Bold, impulsive and seeks adventure

Chinese Horoscopes

RAT
1936 . 1948 . 1960 . 1972 . 1984 . 1996 . 2008 . 2020
Humorous, honest, meticulous and hardworking

OX
1937 . 1949 . 1961 . 1973 . 1985 . 1997 . 2009 . 2021
Intelligent, self confident, patient and trustworthy

TIGER
1938 . 1950 . 1962 . 1974 . 1986 . 1998 . 2010 . 2022
Courageous, a natural leader, passionate and independent

RABBIT
1939 . 1951 . 1963 . 1975 . 1987 . 1999 . 2011 . 2023
Peace loving, polite and intelligent, with artistic tendencies

DRAGON
1940 . 1952 . 1964 . 1976 . 1988 . 2000 . 2012 . 2024
Intuitive, artistic, lucky and successful

SNAKE
1941 . 1953 . 1965 . 1977 . 1989 . 2001 . 2013 . 2025
Philosophical, wise, calm and elegant

HORSE
1930 . 1942 . 1954 . 1966 . 1978 . 1990 . 2002 . 2014
Cheerful, popular, independent, an adventurer at heart

SHEEP
1931 . 1943 . 1955 . 1967 . 1979 . 1991 . 2003 . 2015
Good natured and generous with a good mind for business

MONKEY
1932 . 1944 . 1956 . 1968 . 1980 . 1992 . 2004 . 2016
Witty, inventive, a fast learner with an excellent memory

ROOSTER
1933 . 1945 . 1957 . 1969 . 1981 . 1993 . 2005 . 2017
Hardworking, social and confident, family oriented

DOG
1934 . 1946 . 1958 . 1970 . 1982 . 1994 . 2006 . 2018
Honest, faithful, responsible and prosperous

PIG
1935 . 1947 . 1959 . 1971 . 1983 . 1995 . 2007 . 2019
Sensitive, cultured, diligent, a perfect friend

ANNE GEDDES®

www.annegeddes.com

ISBN: 978-1-921652-19-6 - Pure Nest Cover
ISBN: 978-1-921652-20-2 - Moth Orchid Cover

First published in 2010 by Anne Geddes Publishing
Geddes Group Holdings Pty Ltd
Registered Office, Level 9, 225 George Street
Sydney 2000, Australia

Images, sketches and quotes by Anne Geddes

Designed by Claire Robertson
Produced by Kel Geddes
Printed in China by 1010 Printing International Limited, Hong Kong